The
Little Red Book
Of
Stuff That Works!

The Little Red Book Of Stuff That Works!

Advice, instructions, suggestions, ideas,
thoughts, observations, principles, questions,
considerations, truths, notions, hints, philosophies,
theories, witticisms, opinions, quotations
and other great stuff that works!

by

Larry H. Winget

The Little Red Book Of Stuff That Works!

Larry Winget
Copyright © MCMXCIV

Printed in the United States of America.
Cover design and typesetting by Ad Graphics, Tulsa, Oklahoma.
ISBN: 1-881342-04-2
Library of Congress Catalog Number: 94-90338

"The Little Red Book Of Stuff That Works™" is a trademark of Win Publications!,
Win Seminars!, and Larry Winget, denoting a series of books and products
including pocket cards, calendars, audio cassettes and videotapes.

Published by:
Win Publications!
a subsidiary of Win Seminars!, Inc.
P.O.Box 700485 • Tulsa, Oklahoma 74170
918 745-6606

Order information:
Call Toll Free:
800 749-4597

Dedication

This book is dedicated to my sons, Tyler and Patrick.

To Tyler for his sense of humor, his quick wit, his undying enthusiasm and his continuous passionate search for a good time.

To Patrick for his thoughtfulness, his kindness, his sensitivity, his creativity and his goodness.

I hope that the words in this book serve them well as they grow and become men. As they read these lines, I wish for them laughter, love, wisdom and perspective.

I wish the same for you and yours.

Acknowledgements

It would be impossible to write a book with this many ideas in it and take credit for all of them. While a good portion of these thoughts are indeed just mine, I must admit that many of them were inspired by others. I would love to give credit to each and every person who has inspired me. However, the list would be too long, I would leave someone out and I would probably give credit for the wrong stuff. The fact is that I just can't remember where most of the influence came from to say some of the stuff I have said. So if you read this book and say I've heard ol' what's-his-or-her-name say something real close to that, you are probably right. And by the way, if you **are** ol' what's-his-or-her-name, and recognize some of your stuff, let me say now that I appreciate your contribution and humbly ask your forgiveness for not giving you credit.

and now . . .

Stuff That
Works!

1.

Expect the best.

2.

Be prepared for the worst.

3.

Celebrate it all!

4. **Take responsibility.**

5. **Do more than anyone expects from you.**

6. **Have animals around to love.**

7. **Own a flag and display it proudly.**

8. **Say "Good Morning" and mean it.**

9. Have at least one really good friend.

10. Go to flea markets.

11. Never borrow anything.

12. Go to seminars and hear great speakers.

13. Watch public television.

14. Listen to classical music.

15. Listen to country music every once in a while.

16. "A man is known by the company he avoids."

- Unknown

17. Listen to at least one educational audio series monthly.

18. Never miss an opportunity to vote.

19. Be more black and white in your thinking. There are too many grays in the world as it is.

20.

Become a master "asker."

21. Avoid beating yourself up.

22. Sample all different kinds of food.

23. Never say, "I told you so."

24. Do it now.

25.

Live by the phrase, "Today, not tomorrow."

26. "Success is the progressive realization of a worthy ideal."

   - Earl Nightingale

27. You can't become successful by what you are *going* to do.

28. Dress up for dinner at home once in a while.

29. **Never be intimidated by anyone's title.**

30. **Always try to "out-nice" the other person.**

31. **Try tipping before receiving the service.**

32.

Never tolerate mediocrity.

33. Never compromise. Work toward both parties winning.

34. Buy more really good Halloween candy than you will ever give away and then eat it yourself.

35. "It's not your aptitude but your attitude that determines your altitude." - Reverend Jesse Jackson

36. Have an aquarium.

37. Never hang wallpaper with someone you love.

38. **Write your own book just for you that expresses your feelings and beliefs.**

39. **Talk to yourself more.**

40. **"After three days, fish and guests stink."**

                                    - John Lyly

41. Find a great "handy-man" and pay him well.

42. Find a plumber you can trust.

43. Find an electrician who bills by-the-job.

44. Find an attorney you can trust.

45. **Find a really good insurance agent.**

46. **Find an auto mechanic who will fix what needs to be fixed at the price promised.**

47. **Find a minister who really loves people.**

48. Watch less television.

49. Play more games.

50. Remember that "no one succeeds alone." You need others.

51. Money comes to you as it goes from you.

52. Be early.

53. Do things faster than is expected.

54. Buy yourself a birthday present.

55. "The future belongs to those who believe in the beauty of their dreams."
— **Eleanor Roosevelt**

56. Send a love letter to yourself.

57. Laugh a lot!

58.

Live life as if you were an exclamation point!

59. **Make decisions quickly. If you make a bad one, you'll know sooner and can make another one.**

60. **Never allow anyone to waste your time.**

61. **Have a good handshake.**

62. **Forgive.**

63. **Paint your house often, the change will do you good.**

64. **Use big thick towels.**

65. **Get a massage regularly.**

66. **Keep your car clean inside and out.**

67. **Answer all correspondence immediately.**

68. **Treat employees and friends like volunteers.**

69. "Unless life is lived for others it is not worthwhile."

    - Mother Teresa

70. Be nice to telephone solicitors. They are only doing their job.

71. Beware of places that sell "new" antiques.

72. **Drink really good coffee.**

73. **Avoid instant coffee.**

74. **Never trust anyone who tells you that you won't be able to tell the difference.**

75. **You have to be before you can do, and you have to do before you can have.**

76. **Never let the telephone interrupt meals, baths, playing with your kids, or making love.**

77. **Park your car outside of a bakery and enjoy the smells.**

78. **Keep your shoes shined.**

79. **Hug more.**

80. **Don't be so skeptical.**

81. **Give away ten percent of your gross income.**

82. **Save ten percent of your gross income.**

83. **Read <u>The Greatest Salesman In The World</u> by Og Mandino.**

84.

Teach your dog good manners.

85. **Go to a Christmas Eve candlelight service.**

86. **Listen to Christmas music all year.**

87. **"Whatever you vividly imagine, ardently desire, sincerely believe, and enthusiastically act upon must inevitably come to pass."**
    - Paul J. Meyer

88. **Avoid fast food whenever possible.**

89. **Read at least one book every month.**

90. **Smile more than you think you need to.**

91. **Leave every situation better than you found it.**

92.

Eat dessert first.
Life is too short.

93. **Avoid anything sold on television for $19.95.**

94. **Never buy Gin-Su anything.**

95. **Always have plenty of tape on hand.**

96. **When in doubt, eat chocolate.**

97. **Never run out of cereal.**

98. **Become a "Reverse Paranoid."**

99. **Read books of quotations.**

100. **Become a good speller.**

101.

"The-deal-of-a-lifetime" — rarely is.

102. **"The more you help others, the greater your own success will be."**
                              - A. L. Williams

103. **Do more.**

104. **Talk less.**

105. **Learn to dance.**

106. **Live by The Law of Sowing and Reaping.**

107. **Read biographies.**

108. **You must see it first in your mind if you are ever going to see it in your reality.**

109. **Own a pair of red socks, and wear them!**

110. **"Even a blind hog finds an acorn every once in a while." - Cowboy**

111. **Be quicker to praise good service than you are to criticize poor service.**

112. Write "I appreciate" notes to your co-workers, your boss, your employees, your friends, your spouse and your kids.

113. " Adversity introduces a man to himself."

- Unknown

114. Give better service than you get.

115. **Only create pictures in your mind of what you do want.**

116. **Remind yourself of your abilities.**

117. **Avoid reminding yourself of your limitations.**

118. **Begin everyday by writing down five things you are thankful for.**

119. **Buy hardback books whenever possible.**

120. **"Heaven never helps the man who will not act."**

                              - Sophocles

121. **Never loan anyone a book. You probably won't get it back.**

122. **Reward your successes.**

123. **Take a public speaking course.**

124. **Take a listening course.**

125. "It's not how good a man shoots that matters. What matters is how willing he is to shoot when there's someone shootin' back at him. A lot are good, few are willing." - John Wayne in <u>The Shootist</u>

126. "You always pass failure on the way to success."

- Mickey Rooney

127. **Believe in your country.**

128. **Believe in others.**

129. **Believe in what you do.**

130. **Believe in what is good, just and right.**

131. **Believe in the future.**

132. **Believe in yourself.**

133. **Believe in something bigger than yourself.**

134. Avoid saying, "I'll try." Saying it is just offering an excuse for not doing it in advance.

135. Look for the good in everyone.

136. Look for the good in everything.

137. "He who hesitates is last."
                            - Mae West

138. Welcome change.

139. Write down your own personal definition of success.

140. Be flexible.

53

141.

Lighten up!

142. Take more risks.

143. Work as hard on yourself as you do your job.

144. Do what you say you are going to do.

145. Never listen to a minister who asks you to think less of yourself than God does.

146. Only associate with people you want to be like, because you will become like those with whom you associate.

147. Be committed.

148. Be proactive.

149. Be real nice.

150.

Stand guard at the door of your mind.

151.

Be the kind of person your dog thinks you are.

152. **Think more.**

153. **"Don't talk about it - Do It!"**
                                     - Grant Gard

154. **Pay your taxes.**

155. **Be yourself. Being someone else is not only frustrating, it's impossible.**

156. Be more flamboyant.

157. "Life is an opportunity for you to contribute love in your own way."
- Bernie Siegel, M.D.

158. Face problems head on. They don't go away by avoiding them.

159. Be an encourager.

160. Make balance a priority.

161. Go to a rodeo.

162. Own a pair of cowboy boots.

163. "Many of life's failures are men who did not realize how close they were to success when they gave up."
- **Thomas Edison**

164. Use sunscreen.

165. Spend as much money on improving your mind as you do on clothes.

166.

Avoid
brown.

167. **Inspect what you expect.**

168. **Always have clean fingernails.**

169. **Make funny faces at the people in the car next to you.**

170. **Never hesitate to exploit opportunities to celebrate.**

171. Care less what others will think when you feel like laughing out loud.

172. Don't embarrass so easily.

173. Avoid secrets.

174. Get rid of clothes that you don't feel your best in.

175. **Learn to juggle.**

176. **"Always do right - this will gratify some people and astonish the rest."**
      - Mark Twain

177. **Never pass a Salvation Army bell ringer without dropping in something.**

178.

Spend more money on fewer things.

179. "The best way to do things is to begin."

                              - **Horace Greeley**

180. Own a speakerphone at your house.

181. Call someone once a week and say, "Thank you for just being you."

182. Read <u>People Magazine</u> only at the dentist's office.

183. Spend more money on dessert than the entree.

184. Be optimistic.

185. Never stay with friends or family when on vacation unless you are willing to reciprocate.

186.

Go Big
Or
Stay Home!

187. **Show up!**

188. **Own a whoopee cushion.**

189. **"Money is not success, but success does include at least *some* money."**
     - Larry Winget

190. **Never wear anything in public that you wouldn't want your best customer to see you in.**

191. **Have good table manners.**

192. **Teach your children manners.**

193. **Never pop your chewing gum.**

194. **Get to movies on time.**

195. **Be quiet once the movie starts.**

196. "The man who doesn't read good books has no advantage over the man who can't read them." - Mark Twain

197. Have fun.

198. Keep your desk clean.

199. Travel lighter than you think you need to.

200. Carry a really good briefcase.

201. Carry a really good pen.

202. Have a good umbrella.

203. Use really good stationery.

204. Never carry on a serious conversation while wearing sunglasses.

205. **Own a yo-yo.**

206. **"Most people would rather die than think; in fact, they do so."**
                    - Bertrand Russell

207. **Put the lid down.**

208. **Avoid all-you-can-eat buffets.**

209. Avoid any place that has more than one "Going Out Of Business Sale."

210. Have a friend named "Cowboy."

211. Be known as a bearer of good news.

212. Always make friends with "the cook."

213. **Rich makes up for a whole lot of ugly!**

214. **Like it or not, you always get results.**

215. **Hold hands with someone you love.**

216.

Hug your kids, even when they think they're too big for it.

217. There is no failure in doing. There is only failure in not doing.

218. Count your items before getting in the express check out line.

219. Have your deposit slip ready before entering the drive-in lane at the bank.

220. **Always accept compliments with a thank you.**

221. **Send flowers to your mother for only that reason.**

222. **Expect challenges.**

223. **Learn how to take ten minute vacations.**

224. Give advice sparingly.

225. Give love freely.

226. Give your time carefully.

227. Give yourself wholeheartedly.

228. Be willing to apologize.

229. Wear seatbelts.

230. Know your next door neighbor.

231. "It is only possible to live happily
     ever after on a day to day basis."
                        - Margaret Bonnano

232. Always ask yourself, "Will this move me closer to where I want to be?"

233. Smile at everyone.

234. Practice good penmanship.

235. Have opinions.

236. **Become a master communicator.**

237. **Avoid contact with negative people.**

238. **Help others win.**

239. **When people ask, "How are you?" Tell them you are terrific. No one wants to hear your problems.**

240.

Be on time.

241.

Start on time.

242.

Stop on time.

243. Never smoke.

244. Be loyal.

245. Be honest.

246. Be ethical.

247. Money is a good thing.

248. **Compliment your kids.**

249. **Say thank you to your spouse for the "ordinary" things.**

250. **You can be in the rat race without being a rat.**

251.

Your best
is
good enough.

252. **Never settle for less than your best.**

253. **Live life to the degree that your tombstone could carry the words, "Empty. All used up."**

254. **Whistle. But don't annoy others with it.**

255. **You don't always get what you pay for.**

256. **Be willing to do the Hard and Necessary, not just the Fun and Easy.**

257. **Ask, "Why not?" more often.**

258. **Learn one new word every day.**

259. **Be an educated consumer.**

260. Eat smart.

261. Avoid full price whenever possible.

262. Know that there is always an alternative.

263. Make sure your lawn is always mowed and your shrubs trimmed.

264. Be the kind of neighbor you would like to live next to.

265. Never let a fat doctor tell you how to lose weight.

266. Never try to lose weight by taking pills.

267. Never underestimate the power of peer pressure.

268. **Take your job seriously, not yourself.**

269. **Return your calls promptly.**

270. **It can always be worse!**

271. **Don't cuss.**

272. **Go on picnics.**

273. **Every night empty your change into a piggy bank. Only rob it for something frivolous and special.**

274. **When the waiter says don't try the _____ , don't.**

275.

When you miss the target, never in history has it been the target's fault.

276. **Never own a radar detector. The speed limits are set to protect us all.**

277. **Never ride with anyone who uses a radar detector. Care about your own safety and the safety of others, even if they don't.**

278.

Call ahead.

279. Never wait for a customer, a salesperson, a doctor, or an attorney longer than twenty minutes. Your time is valuable.

280. Go to New Orleans.

281. Visit lots of different churches.

282. Never say, "I was in the neighborhood so I thought I would drop by." 1. You shouldn't ever just drop by out of respect for other people's time. And 2. People should think they are special enough that you came to visit them on purpose.

283. **Have a list of people you would like to meet. You will be surprised at the opportunities that will present themselves.**

284. **"You will never find time for anything. If you want time you must make it."**

    - Charles Buston

285. **Never say that you gave at the office when you didn't.**

286. **Conserve.**

287. **Never buy a set of encyclopedias. They are outdated the moment they are printed.**

288. **Throw away socks with holes in them.**

289.

Buy things from little kids.

290. Recycle.

291. Be passionate.

292. Surround yourself with things that make you laugh.

293. Buy funny greeting cards.

294. Never throw away old photographs.

295. **Collect something.**

296. **Learn to type.**

297. **Eat raw cookie dough. It's better before you cook it.**

298. **Regardless of what your mother told you, eating raw dough will not give you worms.**

299. Lick the pan when mixing cake frosting, cookies, brownies, or anything chocolate.

300. "Being right half the time beats being half right all the time."

- Malcolm Forbes

301. Have a great library. Your library reflects who you are.

302. Be interested.

303. Be interesting.

304. The more interested you are, the more interesting you will be.

305. Before beginning any project, identify and write down the benefits of accomplishing the project.

306. Before beginning any project, identify and write down the obstacles you will face while working on the project.

307. **Never say anything that you wouldn't want your mother to hear you say.**

308. **Never do anything that you wouldn't want your mother to see you doing.**

309. Read <u>The Ya Gotta's For Success</u> by Larry Winget.

310. Regarding doing business with friends, remember the best way to avoid conflict: Friends Pay Full Price.

311. Never sell your car to anyone you know.

312. "The most valuable of all talents is that of never using two words when one will do."

- **Thomas Jefferson**

313. When talking to small children it is best to be at eye level.

314. Worry is a misuse of the imagination.

315. **Carry only one credit card.**

316. **Learn the value of relaxation.**

317. **You can have as much money as you believe you deserve.**

318. **"Leadership gravitates to the man who can talk." - Lowell Thomas**

319. **Be true to yourself.**

320. **Wear loud ties.**

321. **For higher resale value, drive red or black cars.**

322. **Collect autographs of famous people.**

323. **Practice good posture.**

324. **Have a business card.**

325.

Never
be
dull.

326. **Always carry a business card.**

327. **Listen to educational audio tapes in your car. The average American will spend approximately 19,000 hours in their car. Don't waste it.**

328. **Focus on accomplishment, not activity.**

329. **Throw away all of your To-Do lists. You've got plenty to do without putting it on a list. However . . .**

330. **Have a To-Get-Done list. It's more important to get things done than to do things.**

331. **Don't be too wordy.**

332. **Make up your mind to be happy.**

333. **Never stop learning.**

334. **Earn all you can.**

335. **"Life is like a buffet; you have to serve yourself." - Larry Winget**

336. **Never become so busy with life that you forget to live it.**

337. **Feed your mind as often as you feed your stomach.**

338. **Don't wait for a thousand good ideas before taking action; take action after every good idea.**

339. **Be really fired up about something.**

340. **Do something!**

341. **Be enthusiastic.**

342. **Smiles are reciprocal. If you want one, give one away!**

343. **Think!**

344. "Do not resist change. Without it you become obsolete."

- Larry James

345. Failure is the line of least persistence.

346. Walk!

347. Be a little different. It's the difference that makes the difference!

348. Store garden hoses during the winter.

349. Never go the Post Office on the first day of the month.

350. Never say "with my luck."

351. Develop a sense of urgency.

352. **Be courteous.**

353. **Abundance is an attitude.**

354. **Think prosperous thoughts.**

355. **Feed your pets.**

356. **Respect the rights of others.**

357.

Measure twice.
Cut once.

358. Know why you do things. With a strong enough why you can deal with any how.

359. Don't hesitate to ask for directions.

360. Write things down. Work from document, not from thought.

361. **Avoid television news programs.**

362. **Surprise people.**

363. **"Success is being all you can be in each area of your life without sacrificing your ability to be all you can be in each and every other area of your life." - Larry H. Winget**

364. Support your local zoo.

365. Wear bright colors.

366. Go to used book stores.

367. Life does not give you what you deserve or what you need. Life gives you what you ask for.

368.

Read a really good book on selling. We all succeed in direct proportion to our ability to sell, regardless of our profession.

369. **Find humor wherever you can.**

370. **Never vote for incumbents.**

371. **Never say anything bad about yourself.**

372. **Take children to nice restaurants and teach them how to behave.**

373.

Sit on the floor more. Especially if you have children or pets.

374. Write family members a letter and tell them you love them regardless of past differences.

375. "They conquer who believe they can." - Ralph Waldo Emerson

376. You don't have to be good to start, but you do have to start to be good.

377. **Avoid parking tickets.**

378. **Never buy clothing sold as a set.**

379. **"Walking the tightwire is living; everything else is waiting."**
                              -Karl Wallenda

380. **Never miss an opportunity to say something nice.**

381. What you think about and talk about, comes about.

382. Watch the movie "Old Yeller" every few years, and cry.

383. Dress up for dinner at home once in a while.

384. Wake up enthusiastically!

385. **Make a list of the characteristics, talents and abilities that are uniquely yours.**

386. **Carry a pen and paper. Great thoughts and ideas must be recorded when they occur. Otherwise, they are quickly forgotten.**

387. Take some risks.

388. Give books as presents.

389. Develop good habits.

390. "Speak in terms of your blessings rather than in terms of your challenges." - Catherine Ponder

391.
Love problems. You will be compensated in life in direct proportion to your ability to solve problems.

392. Be careful not to over-cook vegetables.

393. Be as good as your word.

394. Practice doing absolutely nothing.

395. Set goals.

396. Wear hats during the winter.

397. Don't waste time carrying a grudge.

398. "Follow your bliss."
                                    - Joseph Campbell

399. Always take time for your children.

400. Watch a video of The Little Rascals.

401.

Ask a little, get a little. Ask a lot, get a lot.

402. See the Lincoln Memorial.

403. Carry a pocket knife.

404. Look for solutions.

405. Write your legislators.

406. Define expectations clearly in advance.

407. Follow up.

408. **Happiness is a choice.**

409. **Know how to cook.**

410. **Be known for something.**

411. **Have a "smile thing." (Something that makes you smile whenever you think about it.)**

412.

Study success.

413. Use things and love people. Not the reverse.

414. "Man cannot live by bread alone; he must have peanut butter."

- Unknown

415. Protect your reputation at all costs.

416. Money is a measuring stick.

417. Know how to play.

418. Fill your mind with the pure, the powerful, the positive, and the prosperous.

419. "On with the dance - let the joy be unconfined." - Mark Twain

420. Never "knock" anyone for any reason.

421. **Be coachable.**

422. **Savor success.**

423. **Never apologize for winning.**

424. **Never be boastful.**

425. **You can't be like everyone else and stand out in the crowd.**

426. "Success does not come from doing any extraordinary thing. Success comes from doing ordinary things extraordinarily well."

- Unknown

427. Prosperity is a state of mind.

428. Never underestimate the difference you can make.

429. **Greet people enthusiastically.**

430. **Call people by their names.**

431. **Use good grammar.**

432. **Remember that all the money you are ever going to have is currently in the hands of someone else.**

433.

When it quits being fun - quit!

434. "If you want something you have never had, you have to do something you have never done."

- Mike Murdock

435. Never let someone who is broke tell you how to become rich.

436. You alone hold the key to your future.

437. Be able to laugh at yourself.

438. Spend twice as much time rinsing the soap off your car as you do putting the soap on your car.

439. Have regular medical checkups.

440. Exercise!

441.

Remember the "Hole Principle". When you find yourself in one, stop digging!

442. **Depend on yourself.**

443. **It is sometimes easier to beg forgiveness than it is to ask permission.**

444. **Floss.**

445. **Avoid people wearing overcoats in the summer.**

446. **When you find yourself on a dead horse, get off!**

447. **When pointing the finger of blame, aim it at yourself, then move on! Instead of fixing blame, fix the problem.**

448. **Learn to say no.**

449. **Attitude is contagious. Is yours worth catching?**

450. **Never get a tattoo.**

451. "We ought not to look back unless it is to derive useful lessons from past errors, and for the purpose of profiting by dear-bought experience."
- George Washington

452. If you drink, don't drive.

453. Don't mess with Texas.

454. **Brush your teeth three times a day, and visit the dentist regularly.**

455. **Never put "just" or "only" in front of your name or any description of who you are or what you do.**

456. **Take all you want, but eat all you take.**

457. The best way to determine whether to do or not to do something is to look at the consequences of not doing it. No consequences? Skip it. Big consequences? Do it.

458. Use black ink.

459.

Wherever you are, be there.

460. "The quality of a persons life is in
     direct proportion to their
     commitment to excellence regardless
     of their chosen field of endeavor."
                              - Vince Lombardi

461. Beware of "some assembly
     necessary."

462. A rut is a grave with both ends kicked out.

463. "Irregardless" is not a word.

464. Don't litter.

465. Look like you are "on purpose."

466. Take notes.

467. **Why not you!**

468. **Get smarter.**

469. **"If you want to win anything - a race, your self, your life - you have to go a little berserk." - George Sheehan**

470. **Enjoy.**

471. **Share.**

472. When you use the word "but" it negates everything said up until then.

473. Your goals are more important than anyone's opinions of your goals.

474. Ask lots of questions.

475. Forgive yourself anytime for anything.

476.

ALWAYS
beware of people who
ONLY
speak in absolutes.
NEVER forget that!

477. **Expand your comfort zone.**

478. **The best way to start is to start.**

479. **Avoid buying matching ties and pocket squares.**

480. **You can ALWAYS change!**

481. **Never underestimate the power of your words.**

482. **The words you use will leave an indelible mark on the hearer.**

483. **The words you say can and will be used against you.**

484. **Things don't get better until you do.**

485. **Do what you love. Love what you do.**

486. **Don't make promises you don't plan to keep.**

487. **"Do or do not. There is no try."**
                                            - Yoda

488. **Develop a belief system of serving and loving others through your life, your love, your words, your product and service, and great quantities of money will come.**

489. **Go a little bit crazy.**

490. **Learn to pray.**

491. True prayer begins when you encounter a situation where learned words do not fit.

492. "Seek ye first the kingdom of heaven, and the Masaratti will get here when it's supposed to."
    - Marianne Williamson

493. One step at a time. Just one step at a time.

494. "Money is a terrible master but an excellent servant." - P. T. Barnum

495. Don't tell me what you are going to do, show me what you have done.

496. Live more!

497. Stop. Look. Listen.

498. Amounts are never enough. Only your best is enough.

499. Read the Bible.

500. Create memories.

501. The greatest plan in the world won't work if you won't.

502. **Fall in love with your plan for accomplishing goals. It is the plan and not the goal that you are faced with daily.**

503. **It's not what happens to you that matters. It's what you do about what happens to you that matters.**

504. **Never mistake motion for progress and movement for acheivement.**

505. **"Don't curse the darkness - light a candle."**

                              - Chinese proverb

506. **Concentrate on the basics.**

507.

Never confuse what you CAN do with what you WILL do.

508. **Do what winners do and your chances of being a winner will be dramatically increased.**

509. **Do what losers do and your chances of being a loser are guaranteed.**

510. **The customer is always right.**

511. **Results are a product of action.**

512. **In order to change what you have, change what you are.**

513. **"Opportunity does not linger, nor does it pause to look back."**

      - Jim Rohn

514.

Results.
That's the
only thing.

515. **Your actions either move you closer to where you want to be or farther from where you want to be.**

516. **No action is neutral.**

517. **Never neglect the details.**

518. **The book you do not read will not help you.**

519. Marriage is not a 50-50 proposition. It is 100-100.

520. "Wisdom is the quality of being able to make the right use of knowledge."
- Tim Hansel

521. You earn slack.

522. Live every day as if it is going to be your last.

523. When you have finished your day, be done with it.

524. Avoid clutter.

525. Nature abhors a vacuum.

526. Do all you possibly can!

527. Seize the day!

528. Never eat blue food.

529.

Forget luck.

530. Watch nature programs on television.

531. Travel all you can, wherever you can, whenever you can.

532. The only thing constant is change.

533. "Show me a good loser and I'll show you a loser." - Jimmy Carter

534. **Timing is the key.**

535. **Buy this book for a friend.**

536. **Shake things up.**

537. **"Read odd stuff. Visit odd places. Make odd friends. Hire odd people. Cultivate odd hobbies. Work with odd partners." - Tom Peters**

538.

After all is said and done, more is said than done.

539. Be a sponge for knowledge.

540. Keep it in the right perspective.

541. Cancel all negative thoughts with positive ones.

542. Pay your bills happily.

543. **End every day by making a list of what must be accomplished tomorrow.**

544. **Practice does not make perfect. Practice makes permanent.**

545. **"Impossible is a word to be found in the dictionary of fools."**
     - Napoleon

546. Be known as "the one who gets things done."

547. Set goals as a family.

548. "The chains of habit are too weak to feel until they are too strong to break." - Unknown

549. Stretch yourself: physically- mentally - spiritually.

550.

Aim high.

184

551. **Think like a winner, act like a winner and look like a winner. People love to do business with winners!**

552. **Sometimes the light at the end of the tunnel is a train.**

553. **Be brief, clear and specific when communicating ideas.**

554.

Make other people feel important.

555. Protect the sanctity of your home.

556. Don't make a habit of bringing work home. Do work stuff at work.

557. It came to pass . . . it didn't come to stay!

558. Be persistent.

559. **Admit your mistakes. Never try to cover them up or pass the buck.**

560. **Do more than you are paid to do and you will eventually be paid more for what you do.**

561. **Don't allow too much time to do things. Work always expands to the time alloted.**

562. It is easier to pay taxes on the money you have, than to pay no taxes on the money you don't have.

563. Be slow to judge people.

564. Avoid strangers who begin conversations with, "Hey. Can I talk to you for a minute?"

565.

You don't have to be good to start, but you do have to start to be good.

566. Be careful of people collecting money door-to-door.

567. When a charitable group calls asking for money, ask them to send you a financial statement showing how much of the donation actually goes for the cause.

568. Go barefoot more often.

569. **Take ten deep breathes three times daily. It's good for you.**

570. **Send birthday cards.**

571. **Buy yourself a toy.**

572. **"Keep your money circulating. If you hoard it for a rainy day, you may have to spend it on an ark."**

- John Randolph Price

573. Never admit that you don't believe in Santa Claus.

574. "No one gets very far unless he accomplishes the impossible at least once a day."

- Elbert Hubbard

575. Ignorance is more contagious than intelligence.

576. You are a reflection of what you see, what you hear, and the people you associate with.

577. The most damaging words you will ever hear will come from you.

578. "Life is too short to be little."
- **Disraeli**

579. **When faced with a dilemma: Stay for all you are worth. Give it your very best. Explore all options. Then give yourself permission to let go and move on.**

580. **Don't over commit.**

581. **Pick your battles. Some things really aren't worth fighting over.**

582. Spend more time on doing the right thing instead of doing things right.

583. Enjoy the differences in people.

584. The best way to predict the future is to create it.

585. Scope up!

586.

**When you're green,
you're growing.
When you're ripe,
you're rotting.
When you're blue,
you're through.**

587. **Avoid all animals named Killer.**

588. **Appreciate the beauty in nature.**

589. **"Any fool can criticize, condemn, and complain - and most do."**
— **Dale Carnegie**

590. **Return your telephone calls promptly.**

591. When someone tells you what you can't do — RUN!

592. "If you're not ready to run with the big dogs, don't get off the porch." - Cowboy

593. "You would be surprised at what you can observe, just by looking around."
                                                    - Yogi Berra

The Little Red Book of Stuff That Works!

594.

A guaranteed way to avoid criticism:

Say nothing.
Do nothing.
Be nothing.

595. **If you are going to go through life looking in the rearview mirror, do it in a red Porsche convertible.**

596. **Always carry a one hundred dollar bill.**

597. **You must first see it in your mind if you are ever going to see it in your reality.**

598. It is a mistake to say, "Things couldn't possibly get any worse." Things can always get worse!

599. Success is not only your right, it is your obligation!

600. "Fortune favors the bold." - Virgil

601. Choose excellence!

602. **Never underestimate your ability to accomplish the impossible.**

603. **Don't overwater your houseplants!**

604. **One of the keys to time management is the effective use of the trash can.**

605. **When in doubt, throw it out.**

606. **Everyone you meet can teach you something.**

607. **"You give but little when you give your possessions, it is when you give of yourself that you truly give."**
     - Kahlil Gibran

608. **Tomorrow may be too late.**

609. **WHAT you are is not WHO you are.**

610. **Fine-tune your telephone skills.**

611. **Say YES!**

612. **Do the big stuff first.**

613. **Ask yourself, "What is the most valuable use of my time right now?"**

614. **What goes around comes around.**

615. **Be good to your parents.**

616. **Be spontaneous!**

617. **Never, never, never wear a toupee!**

618. **Accept that the clothes dryer will eat only one of your favorite pair of socks.**

619. **Become comfortable speaking in front of groups.**

620. **They don't ask how. They ask how many.**

621. "I don't believe you are put here to make a living. I believe you are put here to live your making and by living your making, you will make your living."

- Les Brown

622. Everything will cost more than you budget.

623. "Live juicy!" - Sark

624. **Everything takes longer than you planned.**

625. **Amaze everyone.**

626. **Be unique.**

627. **Take naps in the afternoon.**

628. **Read outloud.**

629. **Stay loose.**

630. **Make up a recipe for cookies.**

631. **Have a humongous bathrobe.**

632. **Build tents in your house out of chairs and blankets.**

633. **Own a good sleeping bag.**

634. "Go confidently in the direction of your dreams. Live the life you have imagined." - Henry David Thoreau

635. See the giant redwoods in California.

636. Visit the Grand Canyon.

637. Spend time with yourself.

638.

People are not the only thing. People are everything.

639. Focus on BEING more than DOING.

640. What you do is an outgrowth of what you are.

641. Study the low bid very carefully before accepting it.

642. Tell someone you love them . . . TODAY!

643. **Prepare for the future. You are going to spend most of your life there.**

644. **Have a Plan B.**

645. **"It is better to be prepared for an opportunity and not have one than to have an opportunity and not be prepared."**

- Whitney Young

646.

"There is no box made by God nor us but that the sides can be flattened out and the top blown off to make a dance floor on which to celebrate life!"

- Kenneth Caraway

647.

Elvis has left the building.

Larry Winget

Larry Winget knows what he's talking about! He has extensive experience in both the large and small business environments. He worked with AT&T and Southwestern Bell for over a decade and has owned three of his own businesses. He has experienced both incredible business success as well as total business failure. However, Larry is proof that you can go belly-up in business without going face-down in failure!

Larry now travels the country delivering speeches and seminars in the areas of Success, Prosperity, Sales, Leadership, Teambuilding, and Being Customer Focused. He is a member of the National

Speakers Association, a charter member and past president of the Oklahoma Speakers Association, and the founder of Win Seminars!

Larry is an author, speaker, consultant, trainer and entrepreneur. His unique combination of simple, straightforward, high-impact principles combined with humor and enthusiasm make his material fresh, fun and easy to apply.

His stories of his friend Cowboy, his dogs Elvis and Nixon, and Tarzan, Superman, and The Lone Ranger are classics that will make you laugh, cry and inspire you to succeed and keep life in the right perspective!

For more information on Larry's many books, tapes, speeches or seminars contact:

Win Seminars!
P. O. Box 700485
Tulsa, OK 74170
800 749-4597